Sukhoi Su-27 SM(3)/SKM

Multifunctional Strike Fighter from Amur

HUGH HARKINS

Copyright © 2016 Hugh Harkins

All rights reserved.

ISBN: 1-903630-63-0
ISBN-13: 1-903630-63-1

Sukhoi Su-27 SM(3)/SKM

Multifunctional Strike Fighter from Amur

© Hugh Harkins 2016

Published by Centurion Publishing
United Kingdom

ISBN 10: 1-903630-63-0
ISBN 13: 978-1-903630-63-1

This volume first published in 2016
The Author is identified as the copyright holder of this work under sections 77 and 78 of the Copyright Designs and Patents Act 1988

Cover design © Centurion Publishing & Createspace

Page layout, concept and design © Centurion Publishing

All rights reserved. No part of this publication may be reproduced, stored in a retrieval system, transmitted in any form, or by any means, electronic, mechanical or photocopied, recorded or otherwise, without the written permission of the publisher

The publisher and author would like to thank all organisations and services for their assistance and contributions in the preparation of this volume. JSC Sukhoi Design Bureau (Sukhoi Aviation Holding Company), KnAAPO (Komsomolsk-on-Amur Aircraft Production Association), United Aircraft Corporation, MMPP Salut, NPO Saturn, JSC V. Tikhomirov NIIP, Zhukovsky, JSC Tactical Missiles Corporation, JSC Concern Radio-Electronic Technologies (KRET), JSC Ramenskoye Design Bureau (RPBK), Rostec Corporation, NPP Zvezda, Gromov Flight Research Institute and the Ministry of Defence of the Russian Federation

CONTENTS

	INTRODUCTION	i
1	FROM SUKHOI T-10 - Su-27S/SK	3
2	Su-27SM(3)/SKM	17
3	OPERATIONAL AIRCRAFT AND UNITS	49
4	APPENDICES	77
5	GLOSSARY	81

INTRODUCTION

The purpose of this volume is to detail the Sukhoi Su-27SM(3)/SKM family of 4th+ generation multirole combat aircraft which emanated from an upgrade program for serial production Su-27S 4th generation air superiority fighter aircraft and a new build program for Su-27SKM and Su-27SM3 aircraft for the export and domestic markets respectively.

The volume covers the evolution of the first generation Su-27 air superiority fighter, which was born out of the T-10 development program of the 1970's, leading to the 21st century Su-27SM(3)/SKM multirole combat aircraft through the anomaly that was the Su-30KI development of the late 1990's. No attempt is made to detail the plethora of developments that evolved from the Su-27 such as the two-seat Su-30 families, attention being fixed on the further development of the single-seat Su-27S into the Su-27SM(3)/SKM variants.

All technical information regarding the aircraft, systems and weapons have been provided by the respective developers/manufacturers, as have many of the photographs and graphics. Certain elements of text, when pertinent, are taken from the volumes 'Sukhoi Su-35S 'Flanker' E, Russia's 4++ Generation Super-Manoeuvrability Fighter' and 'Sukhoi Su-30MKK/MK2/M2 - Russo Kitashiy Striker from Amur'.

1

FROM SUKHOI T-10 - SU-27S/SK

From November 2015, western media reports made continual references to the air defence and strike operations of Russian Federation Air Force (part of the Aerospace Forces) Sukhoi Su-27SM 4th+ generation multirole fighter aircraft serving with the Russian Aerospace Group based at Hmeymim air base, Latakia, in the Syrian Arab Republic; the Aerospace Group being tasked with conducting air strikes on opposition forces, including ISIS (Islamic State) and affiliated groups, in Syria in support of the Syrian Arab Republic military. Reports of Su-27SM numbers operating from the base ranged from as little as four to a full squadron strength detachment of twelve such aircraft. Despite their being a complete absence of visual evidence or a document trail regarding such a deployment, reports of this apparent Ghost Squadron continued unabated, despite having no basis in fact, unless of course Russia had perfected paraxial ray optics or optical spatial cloaking – using the principles of Fourier optics to alter light beams to produce visible spectrum stealth – in short bending light beams away from an object to make it seem invisible. The truth of course was far less dramatic, it simply being a fact that no such deployment had taken place, the Su-27SM's remaining firmly within the borders of the Russian Federation; the only acknowledged Su-27SM operation in support of the Russian campaign over Syria being a four aircraft escort force for Su-34 strike aircraft transiting down the Caspian Sea en-route to Syria via Iran and Iraq.

The Su-27SM, and its export analogue the Su-27SKM, constitute a multipronged program to introduce an updated, multirole variant of the first generation Su-27S air superiority fighter for service in the first few decades of the 21st century, in both Russian domestic and export service. The program underwent several phases in which in-service Su-27S fighters were upgraded for the Russian Federation Air Force under several contracts, together with a new build variant designated Su-27SM3, which entered Russian Federation service in 2011. The export variant met with only limited success, Indonesia purchasing a token force of three new build aircraft to operate alongside its earlier purchase of Su-27SK air superiority fighters and Su-

30MK2 two-seat multirole strike fighters, the latter type purchased over two separate contracts. There are, however, large numbers of Su-27S/SK remaining in service with several air forces worldwide, it remaining possible that some of these fleets may eventually go through an SM type upgrade, it, of course, being just as likely that these could be replaced by new generation aircraft in the mould of the Su-30MKI/SM or the 4th++ generation Su-35S supermanoeuvrable multifunctional strike fighters.

Development of the Su-27SM/SKM (SKM demonstrator Black 305 above) saw the first generation Su-27 evolve into a viable multirole fighter aircraft for service in the first few decades of the 21st century. UAC

The design origins of the Su-27SM/SKM fighter family go back to the Sukhoi Su-27S program, the origins of which go back to the original Sukhoi T-10 dating back to the early 1970's, design work on which had actually commenced under the leadership of O.S. Samoilovich in late 1969, when the Sukhoi OBK Design Bureau in the then Soviet Union had initiated studies into concepts for a new generation long range air superiority fighter intended for service with the Soviet IA-PVO (*Istrebitelnaya Aviatsiya Protivo-Vozdushnoy Obstrany*/Air Defence Force).

It was decided from the onset that the new fighter would be optimised for the primary air superiority mission, albeit with a stipulation that a secondary ground attack capability would be incorporated. A number of challenging performance goals were stipulated for the new fighter, these including a long operational range and high manoeuvrability, which, combined with modern radar and weapon systems would contribute to meeting the requirement that the new fighter should be capable of engaging and defeating the most modern western fighter aircraft then projected, typified by the McDonnell Douglas (later Boeing) F-15 Eagle air superiority fighter then being developed under the American FX (Fighter Experimental) program.

The Su-27SM3, Red 56 shown above, was a new build variant ordered for the Russian Federation Air Force in August 2009. KnAAPO

During the period 1971-1972, various design houses in the Soviet Union, P.O. Sukhoi, A.I. Mikoyan and A.S. Yakovlev, studied various concept designs, Sukhoi producing a not insignificant number of these in its drive to produce an aircraft unrivalled in its performance class. Among the concepts studied was a conventional design featuring an integral body similar to that seen on the F-15, but this lost out to a concept that placed great importance on widely spaced engines hung under the body of the fuselage, the vertical tail planes being positioned on the fuselage area between the main wings and horizontal tail planes.

Both the Sukhoi and Mikoyan design houses were studying high agility concepts, both arriving at similar configurations, this being attributed to the fact that both utilised data from the same research agency. The design that eventually became the Mikoyan PFI (Advanced Frontline Fighter) Project 9, therefore, resembled a scaled down version of the Sukhoi T-10, the latter being designed around a highly blended fore-body and high lift ogive wing with LERX (Leading Edge Root Extensions).

The initial design for the T-10 was complete by September 1971, submitted for design review in February 1972, and, following the preliminary design review, a number of design revisions were incorporated, following which full-scale development commenced in conjunction with development of a lightweight fighter by Mikoyan; the MiG-29 (Project 9). The Sukhoi and Mikoyan designs were, however, not in competition with each other; the former being planned as a heavy fighter and the latter being planned as a light fighter capable of engaging its NATO

(North Atlantic Treaty Organisation) opposite numbers, later typified by the General Dynamics (later Lockheed Martin) F-16 Fighting Falcon, which was a small/lightweight high agility multirole fighter aircraft, although, in its initial variants, it lacked a medium range radar guided air to air capability.

The driving force behind development of the new Soviet air superiority fighter was to design an aircraft with superior performance and capability to the American FX which led to the McDonnell Douglas F-15A air superiority fighter, which was unchallenged in its capabilities in that role until the advent of the Su-27 in the mid-1980's. USAF

During the course of 1972 to 1973, the T-10 was further redesigned, the changes including increased wing area and fuel capacity. The thrust of the proposed powerplant, A.M. Lyulka (NPO Saturn) AL-31F (Article 99), was increased to compensate for increased weights allowing retention of the design goals for a high thrust to weight ratio which would correspond to increased acceleration, climb rate and manoeuvrability. The new configuration changes underwent rigorous test and evaluation, which included testing large-scale wind tunnel models at the wind tunnel facilities of CAHI, SibNIA and MIA during 1973 to 1974, a change of chief designer on the program being implemented in the former year with the appointment of N.S. Chernyakov.

Detailed design work of the prototype commenced in 1975, by which time the concept, retaining the in-house designation of T-10, was described by Sukhoi as having "an integrated ogive wing configuration, leading-edge root extensions, an all-moving horizontal tail unit mounted on the centre wing section continuation beams, and twin tail fins mounted on engine nacelles at the airframe stern post". The variable engine air intakes were positioned "either side of the plane's roll axis, and suspended from the centre wing section", ensuring a stable air flow to the engines even when the aircraft was flying at high AoA (Angle of Attack), an issue of high importance for the design team in their drive to produce an air superiority fighter with unrivalled agility for an aircraft in its performance class. The configuration was designed to be as compact as possible to reduce weigh in combination with the use of titanium alloys. The undercarriage, a conventional tricycle configuration with single wheel main units and a single wheel nose unit, presented problems for the design team, particularly in regards to finding space for the main unit bays in the compact design. This problem was solved by introducing bays in what Sukhoi described as the "dead air" of the central wing sections, beneath the ducts for the engine air intakes, the retraction process requiring the wheels to be rotated as the units retracted. There was no dedicated air brake installed, the wing flaps doubling as speed brakes.

In the late 1970's and early 1980's, as western intelligence analysts hypothesised over the new Soviet fighters design configuration and capabilities, various artist impressions emerged; this one showing the aircraft armed with older generation air to air missiles, the R-40 (NATO reporting name AA-6 'Acrid') and short range R-60 (NATO reporting name AA-8 'Aphid'), typically carried by the MiG-23 'Flogger', MiG-25 'Foxbat' and Su-15 'Flagon' generation of Soviet Cold War era fighter aircraft, a new generation of very capable air to air missiles being developed for the new Soviet fighters then under development. US DoD

This grainy still (top) of the first prototype of the Sukhoi T-10 design, T-10-1, was amongst the first images of the aircraft to emerge, giving western intelligence agencies a somewhat distorted glimpse of what the new generation Soviet air superiority fighter aircraft looked like. This image confirmed the designs basic layout, but was completely lacking in significant detail that was clearly evident in the much clearer image (above) of the T-10-1 circa 1977.

The T-10 was designed with inherent lateral instability, balanced by an EDCS (Electronic Distance Control System), computerised FBW (Fly-By-Wire) FCS (Flight Control System), the incorporation of which was designed to reduce losses attributed to loss of control and increase the aircraft manoeuvrability in close range air combat. The Soviet Union had pioneered FBW technology with the Sukhoi T-4 intermediate range bomber (cancelled in the 1970's), which conducted its first flight on 22 August 1972. The first American combat aircraft designed with a FBW FCS, the General Dynamics YF-16, conducted its maiden flight on 2 February 1974, followed by the first flight of the European Panavia Tornado prototype (then known as the MRCA - Multi-role Combat Aircraft) on 8 August that year. While the T-4 flew before the YF-16 and Tornado, the FBW FCS installed in the Western aircraft were more advanced than the early Soviet systems, providing FBW control in all axes.

Approval of the T-10 configuration was granted by a decree of the Soviet government on 19 January 1976. Three prototypes (two flight and one ground test) were under construction by the time M.P. Simonov was appointed as the programs chief designer in February 1976, the first, T-10-1, being completed in April 1977 with no less than twelve flying laboratories (test bed aircraft) having flown to test various systems for the aircraft. T-10-1, along with the second, third and fourth development aircraft, T-10-2, T-10-3 and T-10-4, was built at Sukhoi's experimental plant at Zhukovsky near Moscow, the plant at Komsomolsk-on-Amur being appointed as main contractor for serial production of the new fighter.

Western intelligence agencies got their first glimpse of the new Soviet fighter design from photographs taken by a spy satellite while the aircraft was on the ground at Zhukovsky (then known in the west as Ramenskoye). NATO allocated the aircraft the reporting name RAM-K as it was the tenth experimental fighter aircraft observed at the base (the letter I was apparently not used in the RAM reporting sequence).

The prototype T-10, which was powered by a pair of AL-21FZAI afterburning turbojet engines, flew for the first time on 20 May 1977, piloted by Sukhoi Chief Test Pilot V.S. Ilyushin. The AL-21FZAI, which was an interim engine rated at 76.49 kN (16,195 lb.) dry and 109.84 kN (21,692 lb.) in afterburner (the available thrust may have been a little higher than these interim ratings), was a derivative of the AL-21F-3 engine that was used to power a number of Soviet combat aircraft, including the Su-17 and the Su-24 variable-geometry strike aircraft. While the dry thrust of the AL-21F-3 was higher than the dry thrust of the AL-31F (Article 99) planned for the productionised T-10 (Su-27), the afterburner thrust was lower and the engine had a much higher specific fuel consumption compared with the AL-31F; a serious consideration for an aircraft designed as a long-range air superiority fighter.

The conceptual critical design review was passed in October 1977, the aircraft being approved by a committee of the Soviet air forces which was chaired by the 1st Deputy Commander in Chief of the Air Force, Air Marshal A.N. Yefimov. In May 1978, the second flight development aircraft, T-10-2, conducted its maiden flight, this aircraft, like T-10-1, being powered by two AL-21FZAI turbojet engines. In 1979 two further aircraft joined the development program, T-10-3 and T-10-4, both of which were powered by AL-31F afterburning turbofan engines.

Following construction of the initial batch of four aircraft a further five, T-10-5, T-10-6, T-10-9, T-10-10 and T-10-11, were built at the Komsomolsk-on-Amur production plant. As noted above, from the third development aircraft, T10-3, power switched to the more powerful (in afterburner thrust) AL-31F turbofan engine developed to power the series production aircraft. Normal thrust ratings for this engine were given as 79.43 kN (17,857 lb.) dry and 122.59 kN (27,558 lb.) with afterburner. Available information indicates that the AL-31F has a nine-stage HP (High-Pressure) compressor, a four-stage LP (Low-Pressure) compressor and cooled single-stage HP and LP turbines to the rear of the combustor. The efficient air flow afforded by the combination of engine technology, the aircraft air intake design and computer controlled variable inlet guide-vanes, contributed to the Su-27 high performance, conveying varying degrees of capability to conduct extreme high alpha manoeuvres like the 'Cobra' or Tail Slide, without the engines stalling.

A T-10S development aircraft with test R-27 and R-73 air to air missiles. Sukhoi

When it entered service in the 1980's, the high thrust to weight ratio of the AL-31F bestowed upon the standard Su-27S a high maximum speed, unrivalled (for the time) supersonic acceleration, climb rate, and manoeuvrability in certain flight regimes such as sustained turn rate, for an aircraft in its class. Typical engine life was set at around 3,000 hours with a TBO (Time Between Overhaul) of 1,000 hours; reasonable figures for a Soviet era fighter aircraft engine. It should be noted that AL-31F engines have been run for thousands of hours over their scheduled life expectancy during bench test runs.

T-10 development aircraft were accepted for service testing in December 1979. A number of problems with performance goals were encountered during flight tests resulting in the decision to implement a more or less complete redesign to address issues such as controlling weight, reducing drag, increase wing lift and improving roll control. The incomplete T-10-7 was therefore built as the prototype of the new design, receiving the new designation T-10S-1, which in turn received the NATO reporting name 'Flanker' B; the original T-10 design having been allocated the NATO reporting name 'Flanker' A. Sukhoi Design Bureau had to overcome much opposition to the very concept of a redesign, particularly from MIA and the Komsomolsk-on-Amur production plant as series production had already commenced of the fighter with the designation Su-27. This was halted as Sukhoi's argument won through with the support of the Deputy Minister I.S. Silayev, it being clear that the desired superiority over its western counterparts, in particular the F-15, could not be guaranteed with the original T-10 design, therefore, detailed design work on the new fighter design configuration, designated T-10S, was authorised in January 1978. The following year A.A. Kolchin took over design leadership of the program, this being passed to A.I. Knysheb in 1981.

Its combination of high aerodynamic/kinetic performance, high agility, long endurance and combat persistence ensured the Su-27's capabilities would be a real concern for NATO planners. This photograph, taken in the mid-1980's, shows a Su-27 carrying four medium range air to air missiles; two R-27R1 semi-active radar homing and two R-27T1 infrared guided, with two R-27R1's possibly carried on the fuselage centre stations. US DoD

The T-10S-1, which conducted its maiden flight on 20 April 1981, the pilot being V.S. Ilyushin, was more or less a new fighter aircraft design, introducing a new tapered wing with a straight, slatted leading edge flap, flaperon and cropped wingtips incorporating missile launch rails that doubled as anti-flutter weights. The flaperons and differential tailerons replaced the ailerons of the original T-10 design. It was the changes to the fuselage that were most profound, with a shallower, longer drooping nose and deeper spine. The twin vertical tail fin configuration of the T-10 was retained, but this was moved outboard from the original position on top of the engine nacelles to booms, which lay alongside the engines. The main undercarriage door mounted air brakes of the T-10 were replaced by a single spine mounted unit similar to that seen on the F-15 Eagle. The new main undercarriage units were repositioned, as was the nose wheel, which was moved slightly aft.

When the T-10S-1, formerly the incomplete T-10-7, conducted its maiden flight in April 1981, it was clear that it was a new design. However, even with this new design, problems were encountered during flight testing, especially with the new wing design; a solution being found in reducing the wing area of the leading-edge slats.

Three-view general arrangement of the Su-27S/SK configuration. Sukhoi

The new design that would evolve into the production Su-27S (also sometimes referred to as the Su-27P) was equipped with a modern weapons system based around the RLPK-27 weapon control system, featuring a powerful N001 pulse-Doppler radar that was allocated the NATO reporting name 'Slot Back'. This system had a reported detection range of around 240 km, although manufacturer, Tikhomirov NIIP, information suggests 150 km against a fighter size target. The radar can track ten targets simultaneously, but once locked onto a target it could not continue to scan for others. The N001 radar was complemented by an electro-optical complex consisting of an OEPS-27 Electro-Optical Sighting System; an OLS-27 Optical Location System - IRST (Infra-Red Search and Track) and a LR (Laser Rangefinder), allowing the detection, tracking and engagement of targets passively without the need for radar, the emissions of which can betray the host aircraft position. A Shchel HPS (Helmet Pointing System) progenitor to the 21st century HMTDS (Helmet Mounted Target Designation System) allowed engagements of off-boresight targets up to 60° by cueing sensors - the missile tracker head - onto targets that had not been bore-sighted.

Once the design of the new fighter was finalised the Su-27S entered production (the first series production Su-27S conducted its maiden flight on 1 June 1982 [conflicting Sukhoi documentation also states the date as 2 June], piloted by Sukhoi test pilot A.N. Isakov), initial service testing, which finished in December 1983, confirmed the designs expected flight performance superiority over its rivals paving the way for service entry which occurred in June 1985, with the 60th IAP-PVO FAR (Fighter Aircraft Regiment). Although having been in service for over five years the Su-27S was officially signed into service by a decree of the Soviet government on 23 August 1990.

The Su-27 equipped the Russian Knights aerobatic display team from its formation in 1991, remaining so in 2016. The team operates both single-seat Su-27S and the two-seat Su-27UB operational conversion trainer variant (upper aircraft) which conducted its maiden flight in 1984. Sukhoi

Su-27S series production aircraft, which are powered by a pair of AL-31F turbofan engines, each rated at 79.43 kN dry and 122.59 kN with afterburner, have a length of 21.9 m, height 5.9 m and wingspan 14.70 m. Normal take-off weight was set at 23400 kg (Su-27SK) with 2 x R-27R1 (NATO reporting name AA-10 'Alamo'), 2 x R-73 (NATO reporting name AA-11 'Archer') air to air missiles and 5270 kg of fuel. Maximum take-off weight is 30450 kg (Su-27SK). The Su-27S/SK carries 5270 kg of fuel at normal load and 9400 kg at maximum fuel-load. The huge volume of fuel allowed an impressive range to be attained; the aircraft being capable of flying 1340 km at sea level armed with 2 x R-27R1 and 2 x R-73 missiles. In the same configuration, range is 3530 km at altitude. Payload, which can be carried on ten wing and fuselage stations, is, according to Sukhoi information, 4430 kg (other sources suggest around 6000 kg, this being maximum with reduced fuel, while the 4430 kg stated by Sukhoi may be the maximum load carried with maximum fuel), which can include the primary armament of R-27 semi-active radar homing and infrared homing air to air missile variants and R-73 infrared guided air to air missiles, as well as unguided air to surface munitions for the secondary air to surface role.

Following the break-up of the Soviet Union in 1991, the various fleets of aircraft were distributed amongst the former Soviet Republics, the majority going to Russia, but significant numbers going to the other Republics. Here two Ukrainian Su-27's, a single-seater and a two-seat Su-27UB, fly at low level over Ukrainian Sunflower fields with a pair of US ANG F-16C's during exercise Safe Skies 2011. USAF

Although a large heavy fighter the Su-27 showed itself to have an exceptional performance, in many areas, such as range, climb rate, manoeuvrability, in particular its high alpha flight performance, being superior to its rivals. The airframe has a +9 g limit that can be over-ridden by switching the limiter off. Maximum level speed is stated as 1400 km/h at sea level and Mach 2.35 at altitude; climb rate is stated as 19800 meters per minute at sea level, with an operational ceiling of 18500 m.

Following its introduction to service with the air forces of the Soviet Union in June 1985, production continued, with in excess of 500 Su-27's thought to have been produced by the time the Soviet Union began to crumble in 1991. Following the break-up of the Soviet Union in December 1991, the Su-27 remained in service in Russia, assuming greater importance as older aircraft were retired. It is estimated that around 300 Su-27's remain in service in Russia. Smaller numbers of Su-27's equipped the air forces of some former Soviet Republics and new build aircraft were exported to China, Vietnam and Indonesia, while surplus aircraft were exported to several other nations.

While those aircraft inherited by former Soviet Republics were standard Su-27S air superiority fighters, the aircraft delivered to China, Vietnam and Indonesia were the export variant designated Su-27SK, which was basically a Su-27S with some alterations to systems. To fill a requirement for a long-range air superiority fighter, China, in August 1991, had become the first export customer for the Su-27 when that nation ordered 24 Su-27SK/UBK (the export designation for the Su-27S and Su-27UB two-seat operational conversion trainers respectively); the first batch of twelve aircraft, which comprised eight single-seat Su-27SK, and four Su-27UBK two-seat operational trainers, departing Chita in Russia on 27 June 1992, arriving at the PLAAF 3rd Air Division base at Wuhu the same day. The remaining ten Su-27SK and two Su-27UBK's of the initial order were delivered on 8 November 1992, apparently along with a further two aircraft donated by Russia for research and trials work, bringing the number of Su-27's delivered to 26.

The basic Su-27S/SK was designed with a secondary air to surface role, armed with unguided munitions, as evidenced by this Chinese Su-27SK armed with unguided bombs. A driving force behind the Su-27SM/SKM updates was to introduce a true multirole precision strike capability to the first generation Su-27S/SK.

A further batch of 22 aircraft, single and two seat variants, was ordered in early 1995, amendments to contracts, first agreed in 1991, and apparently redrawn in 1993, being made to include licence production of Su-27's at China's Shenyang Aircraft Corporation from kits supplied from Russia; 76 being reported built under the designation J-11 (105 kits were supplied, but it is unclear if all were assembled), the first J-11, assembled from kits produced at KnAAPO, took to the air in December 1998. Deliveries of the second batch, ordered in 1995, commenced that year and were completed in 1996. Deliveries of a further batch of 40 Su-27UBK's, was completed in 2002, bringing the number of Su-27 deliveries from Russia to seventy six. The final number of Su-27's actually acquired/built by China remains something of an enigma; the uncertainty being in regards to the numbers of domestic built J-11 models.

Su-27 White 588, used as a flying laboratory by the Gromov Flight Research Institute and KnAAPO, was involved in testing various equipment in support of the Su-27SM/SKM programs. KnAAPO

Vietnam was the second export customer proper for the Su-27, when, in early 1995, that country ordered a batch of twelve Su-27SK/UBK's, six being delivered later that year with the balance of six Su-27UBK's following in 1996, the aircraft being operated from Phan Rang air base by the 370th Air Division. The Su-27's were joined by successive batches totaling 24 Su-30MK2's.

Indonesia took delivery of two Su-27SK's along with two Su-30MK2 multi-role strike fighters in 2003.

The basic Su-27S airframe spawned a number variants including the Su-27UB two-seat operational conversion trainer, the prototype of which, T-10U-1, flew on 7 March 1984, the naval Su-27K (officially designated Su-33 in 1998), the Su-27M (cancelled in the early 2000's), Su-30M, which led to the multirole Su-30MKI and Su-30MK2 families (the Su-30MK2 family also incorporated much of the design work conducted for the single-seat Su-27M), the Su-34 multifunctional strike fighter and the 4th++ generation Su-35S multidimensional 'super-manoeuvrable' fighter which entered service in 2014. Much of the development work for the Su-30MK2 program fed directly into the Su-27SM/SKM development programs.

2

SU-27SM(3)/SKM

In 2016, the Sukhoi Su-35S $4^{th}++$ generation multidimensional 'super-manoeuvrable' fighter aircraft, which entered operational service in 2014, formed the cutting edge of the Russian Federation Air Force fighter fleet as that service awaited the introduction of the Sukhoi T-50 PAK FA (*Perspektivniy Aviacionniy Complex Frontovoi Aviacii* – Perspective Aviation Complex for Front line Aviation) fifth generation fighter. The introduction of the Su-35S and, under 2016 planning, the T-50 from 2017, are, however, only a few cogs in the wider modernisation of the Russian combat aircraft fleets which included the introduction of other advanced fighter designs – the $4^{th}+$ generation Su-30SM multidimensional 'super-manoeuvrable' fighter, the Su-34 $4^{th}+$ generation multirole strike aircraft, Su-30M2 $4^{th}+$ generation multirole strike fighter, MiG-29SMT front line strike fighter (the Russian Federation Air Force hopes to receive a batch of MiG-35 $4^{th}++$ generation multidimensional fighters, but no such order has materialised as of early 2016) and a small batch of 12 new build Su-27SM3 $4^{th}+$ generation multirole strike fighters developed from the Su-27SM upgrade of first generation Su-27S for domestic service and the new build Su-27SMK developed for the export market.

In the first decade of the 21st century, as funding was not available for any meaningful purchases of new combat aircraft, the Russian Federation Air Force had embarked upon a number of upgrade programs for its tactical combat aircraft fleets leading to the Su-24M2 upgrade of the Su-24M strike aircraft, Su-25SM upgrade of the Su-25 ground attack aircraft, MiG-31BM (ongoing in 2016) upgrade of the Mach 2.83 capable long-range interceptor to multirole standard, and the Su-27SM upgrade of the first generation Su-27S. In the case of the Su-27SM upgrade program this consisted of two contracts, each covering 24 aircraft, featuring an avionics and systems upgrade from Su-27S(II) standard to Su-27SM standard, the last batch of which, procured under the State Defence order for 2009, was delivered to the 22nd GvIAP (Guards Aviation Fighter Aircraft Regiment) in Primorsky Territory in late November 2009.

For a brief period, from 2011 until 2013, the Su-27SM3 could lay claim to be the most advanced operational single-seat variant of the prodigious Su-27 extended family in service with the Russian Federation Air Force. KnAAPO

The Su-27SM upgrade for the Su-27S in domestic Russian service was developed alongside the Su-27SKM developed for the export market as an upgrade of existing Su-27SK or new build, there being a number of differences between the Su-27SM and the Su-27SKM in regards to systems, the Su-27SKM also being available with an in-flight refuelling capability lacking on the Su-27SM, this being the major structural difference between the two variants, the new build Su-27SM3 being structurally distinct from both the Su-27SM and Su-27SKM variants.

The road to the Su-27SM/SKM had been paved by the one-off Su-30KI prototype, which, while certainly it could be considered an anomaly in regards to its designation, was, according to KnAAPO documentation going back to 1998, "an upgraded variant of the Su-27SK", despite its Su-30KI label, the aircraft, which appeared with the '27' code on the forward fuselage, having no more in common with the two main Su-30 families, the two-seat Su-30MKI/MKM/MKI(A)/SM series and the Su-30MKK/MK2/M2 series, than their common Su-27 ancestry.

The major difference between the Su-30KI, the prototype of which conducted its maiden flight on 28 June 1998, and the Su-27SK, according to KnAAPO documentation, was the inclusion of an enhanced avionics suite in the Su-30KI – GPS (Global Positioning System), VOR (Very High Frequency Omnidirectional Range) and DME (Distance Measuring Equipment) and incorporation of a retractable in-flight refueling system on the port side forward fuselage just below the windscreen, which apparently had no effect on the OLS (Optical Location Station) sensor ball, which, as with the Su-27S, remained in the central position just ahead of the aircraft windscreen whereas in other members of the Su-27/30 family so equipped, necessitated the OLS sensor being offset to starboard. Enhancements to the Tikhomirov NIIP N001 radar system allowed the application of new advanced weapons such as the RVV-AE active radar guided air to air missile and precision guided air to surface munitions.

Going into the second half of the 1990's, while IAPA Irkut was forging ahead with its advanced Su-30MKI, KnAAPO, while still committed to development of the S-27M (cancelled in the early 2000's), was pushing ahead with a more conservative enhancement of the first generation Su-27S, this emerging as the Su-30KI. KnAAPO

Initially aimed at an Indonesian requirement for a modern multirole fighter, hopes of any near term order fading even before the aircraft had flown, the Su-30KI was made available to other potential customers, the aircraft being flown at MAKS 99 in August 1999 as part of the Sukhoi marketing drive, and, in November that year, the aircraft was displayed at the LIMA air show in Malaysia. The expected launch customer, Indonesia, would later go on, in the early 2000's, to purchase token batches of two each of Su-27SK and Su-30MK2 fighters and in the second half of the decade a further batch of three Su-30MK2 and a batch of three Su-27SKM, the latter being the Su-30KI's successor as an export Su-27SK enhancement, it certainly being the case that development work conducted on the Su-30KI and the later Su-30MK2, fed directly into the Su-27SM and Su-27SKM programs, the former being the end result of two separate contracts each for the upgrade of 24 serial Su-27S, a third contract covering twelve new build aircraft designated Su-27SM3.

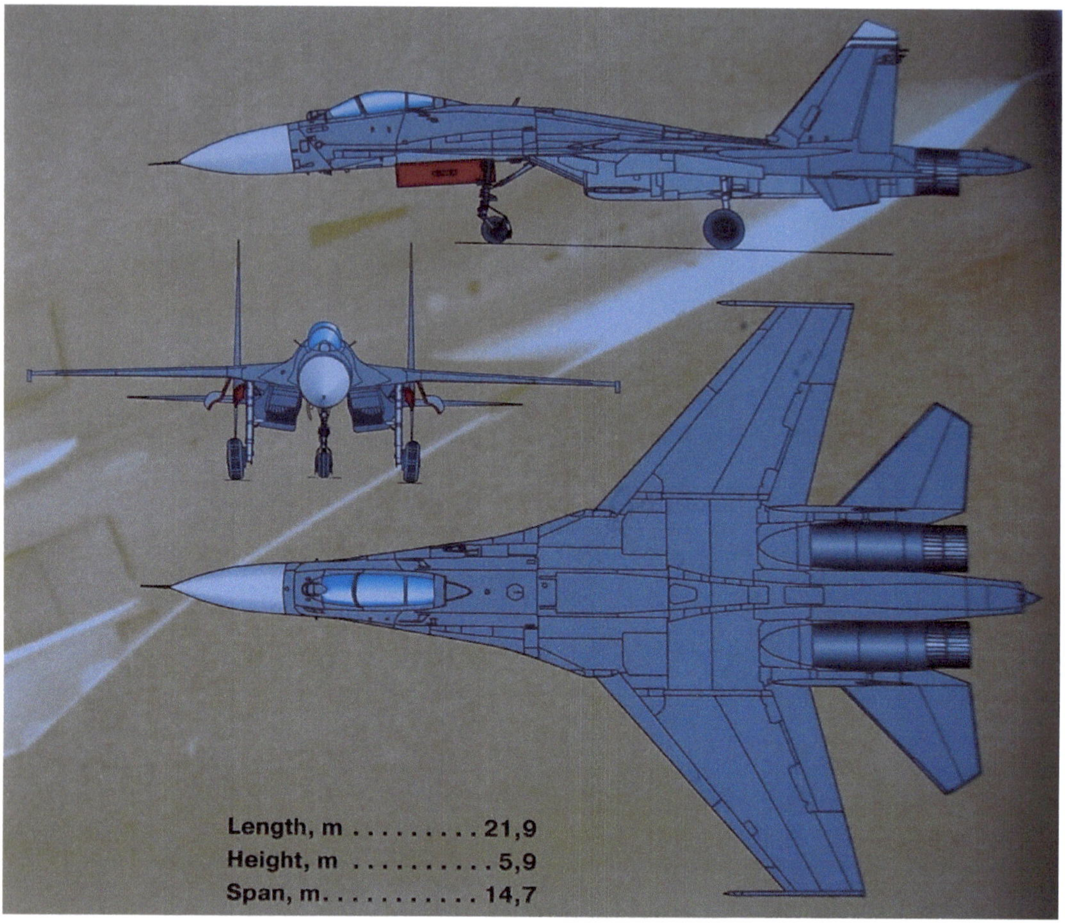

Length, m 21,9
Height, m 5,9
Span, m. 14,7

The major structural difference between the Su-30KI (top) and the Su-27SKM (bottom) was in the location of the OLS sensor ball, which was retained in the centre ahead of the windscreen on the Su-30KI and offset to starboard on the Su-27SKM. KnAAPO/Sukhoi

Model of the Su-27SKM ((Russian Language CKM) development aircraft, Black 305, at one of the many annual and bi-annual international aviation trade shows. KnAAPO

Formerly the Su-30KI demonstrator, in which guise it had conducted its maiden flight on 28 June 1998, Su-27SKM Black 305 was flown in its new incarnation in 2003 as KnAAPO ramped up the Su-27SM/SKM flight development program, which had already gotten underway with the first flight of the Su-27SM prototype, Red 56, in December 2002. Sukhoi

Both the Su-27SM (sometimes referred to as SM1 and SM2 to denote aircraft upgraded under the 1st and 2nd contracts, although they are both referred to as Su-27SM by JSC Sukhoi and KnAAPO) and the Su-27SKM retain the same outward appearance and overall dimensions of the first generation Su-27S/SK, length 21.9 m, height 5.9 m and wingspan 14.7 m, with ten external stores stations, the exception, as noted above, being in the introduction of an in-flight refuelling probe on the Su-27SKM, which, as in other members of the Su-27/30/33 family so equipped, necessitated the OLS sensor, normally located in the centre just ahead of the windscreen, being offset to starboard, this offset position also being introduced on the Su-27SM despite the fact that there is no in-flight refuelling system installed. The Su-27SM3 new build aircraft are distinct from the Su-27SM upgraded aircraft in several respects, not least being the structural strengthening allowing maximum take-off weights of 3 tons higher than their predecessors, allowing an increase to twelve stores stations in line with the number of such stations available on the two respective Su-30 families.

As well as the Su-27SM and Su-27SKM prototype development aircraft, a number of Su-27 flying testbeds were used to flight test some systems for the Su-27SM/SKM and other Su-27/30 derivatives, Su-27 White 588 of the LII, Gromov Flight Research Institute, apparently being utilised in this capacity. GFRI

The twenty four aircraft covered under the first upgrade contract were initially to be powered by overhauled NPO Saturn AL-31F engines with the standard 12500 kgf thrust rating, as were the Su-27SKM aircraft that would be delivered to Indonesia. However, aircraft covered under subsequent contracts would be powered by the improved MMPP Salut AL-31F-M1 (Also known as the AL-31F Series 42 M1) engine with its higher thrust rating of 13500 kgf, this being a deep modernisation of the AL-31F, designed to have only minimal changes overs its predecessors, the AL-31F Series 3, 20 and 23, featuring a number of improvements such as enhanced lift, higher thrust and increased operating life. Despite slightly differing internal vital statistics in comparison to its predecessor, the AL-31F-M1 was designed to fit many Su-27 variants such as the first generation Su-27S, Su-30, Su-33, Su-34 and the Su-27SM family, without the need for any structural modifications to the airframe.

The AL-31F-M1 is a two-shaft by-pass engine featuring, according to JSC Salut, "flow mixture of internal and external ducts behind the turbine, with afterburner common for two ducts and adjustable supersonic, fully variable jet nozzle." Changes compared to the standard AL-31F include the introduction of new materials for rotor parts, introduction of a Digital Full-Authority Engine Regulator which replaced the analogue system of the AL-31F, an improved turbine starter featuring increased power and the capability for startup at higher altitudes, a modernised LPC (Low Pressure Compressor) allowing increased air consumption of 118 kg/s, six kg/s more than that achieved in the AL-31F. Engine thrust, at 13500 kgf, is 1000 kgf higher than the AL-31F, specific fuel consumption remaining the same at 0.685 kg/kgf/h. Overall dimensions and dry weight remained the same as the AL-31F, the AL-31F-M1, however, having an increased diameter inlet of 0.924 m compared with the 0.905 m of the AL-31F. The engine was designed for installation of a thrust-vector control nozzles system as an option, this being flight tested on the LII Su-27, code 05, at the Gromov Flight Research Institute, but not adopted on the Su-27SM.

This Su-27, Blue outline 05 (formerly Red 05), from the Gromov Flight Research Institute, was used as the AL-31F-M1 flying testbed. GFRI

State validation testing for the AL-31F-M1 was completed in 2006, on a modified Russian Federation Air Force Su-27SM, the engine being approved for service in 2007, allowing it to be incorporated into the second contract for 24 Su-27SM upgrades.

AL-31F-M1 (Series 42 M1)

Design: Modular
Maximum thrust: 13500 kgf
Maximum specific fuel consumption: 0.685 kg/kgf/h
Air consumption: 118 kg/s
Inlet diameter: 0.924 m
Maximum diameter: 1140 mm
Length: 4.945 m
Dry weight: 1520 kg
Engine life: 2,000 hours
Platforms: Su-27SM/SM3

The AL-31F-M1 was only the first phase of the AL-31F modernisation drive, phase two resulting in the AL-31F-M2 variant which was aimed mainly at a re-engine program for the Russian fleet of Su-27SM(3) multirole fighters and Su-34 multifunctional strike aircraft. However, by early 2016 these aircraft remained powered by the AL-31F-M1 and AL-31F respectively.

AL-31F-M1 afterburning turbofan. MMPP Salut

In a report dated March 2012, it was confirmed that bench testing, including at the climatic test facility at TsIAM, had been completed, the results showing the engine could attain 14500 kgf static thrust, with further testing achieving the design goal of a 9%, equating to 1215 kgf, thrust increase in flight over that of the AL-31F-M1. Another design goal of the AL-31F-M2 was to reduce specific fuel consumption over the AL-31F/AL-31F-M1, partially through further improvements to the low pressure compressor, combustion chamber and the high pressure turbine. As well as performance improvements over its predecessors, service life of the AL-31F-M2 was increased to 3,000 hours.

The SUU-VEP weapon control system, with the RLPK-27VEP (Article N001VEP) at its centre, was an evolution of the RLPK-27VE installed in the Su-30MKK, which was itself an evolution of the RLPK-27 installed in the Su-27S. V. Tikhomirov NIIP

While the Su-27S/SK were equipped with the N001M and the export standard of that system respectively and the OLS-27 (Article 36Sh) Optical Location Station, the Su-27SM/SKM programs benefitted enormously from development work conducted in connection with the Su-30MK2 two-seat multirole strike fighter program for the export market. This had seen considerable improvements made to the fire control, navigation and data control systems, which built on enhanced capabilities, including enhanced target designation and surface mapping modes and the capability to fire and guide the RVV-AE active radar guided medium range air to air missile, already introduced with the N001VE radar standard equipping the Su-30MKK developed for China, this variant preceding the Su-30MK2, which introduced a new radar standard endowed with additional air to air and air to surface modes, the systems equipping the Su-27SM/SKM being generally the same as the systems installed in the Su-30MK2.

The standard of radar installed in the new build Su-27SM3 is more or less the same as that installed in the earlier upgraded aircraft; that said, Sukhoi documentation would indicate the possibility that there are enhancements, although no specifics have been forthcoming. Sukhoi

An enhanced variant of the SUU-VE equipping the Su-30MKK strike fighters delivered to China's PLAAF, designated SUU-VEP was developed for the Su-30MK2, this also being the standard selected for the Su-27SM/SKM. The SUU-VEP consists of the RLPK-27VEP (Article N001VEP) pulse-Doppler fire control radar, OEPS-27MK (Article 31E-MK) Optical Electronic Sighting System incorporating the OLS-27MK (Article 52Sh) Optical Location Station, SURA-K HMTDS (Helmet Mounted Target Designation System), SILS-27M HUD (Heads up Display) and the 6231R- IFF (Identification Friend or Foe) interrogator.

The developer, V. Tikhomirov NIIP, description of the system reads, "…weapon control system WCS-VEP (SUU-VEP) is intended for air target search, identification and aiming at collision courses and in Tail hemisphere in Look-up and Look-down modes in overwater and overland environment. The given WCS [Weapon Control

System] is mounted on the aircraft of Su-30MK2, Su-27SM types intended to achieve the air superiority, to hit ground and surface targets by means of guided and unguided weapons while group or single actions day-and-night under good or bad weather as well as to fulfill long-range patrolling and tracking." In regards to application, the developer continues, "During combat employment of Su-30MK2 [also corresponds to the Su-27SM] aircraft WCS provides for solution of the following tasks: - turning the aircraft to the area of the assigned target; search, detection, identification, lock-on, auto-tracking, coordinate and parameter measurement of air targets; aiming, generation of target designation & weapon and aircraft control commands and signals; air target hitting by means of guided missiles with RHH and IRHH and built-in guns; en-route flight and turning to programmed ground target in the given direction."

The following data, provided by Tikhomirov NIIP, pertains to the standard of WCS fitted in the Su-27SM:

"'Air-to-Air', 'Air-to-Ground' weapon control system WCS-VEP (Sh101VEP) provides for application of the following weapons: RVV-AE, R-27ER1, R-27R1, R-27ET1, R-27T1, R-27EP1, R-27P1, R-73E, X-31A, X-59MK, X-35E, air bombs, unguided missiles, GSh-301."

"Radar aiming complex includes: RLPK-27VEP ((N001VEP) for the following weapon application: R-27P1, R-27EP1, X-59MK, X-35E."

"On-board digital computer (BTsVM-900), duel channel digital receiver – N001-03VP2; "Digital processor – Baget 55-04.02; Intermediate frequency signal switchboard – N001-39; master oscillator N001-22P; bus adapter switch N001-04M'"

"Radar type, Pulse Doppler; Pulse repetition frequency, high, medium, low."

"In 'Air to Air' mode the radar provides as follows: velocity search; search with ranging; air target illumination and transmission of radiocorrection commands to control missiles with radar homing heads; to control missiles with infrared homing heads; search, lock-on and tracking of visually visible target in close combat; target IFF; operation in adversary EW [Electronic Warfare] environment; jammer coordinate measurement; interaction with ECM [Electronic Counter Measures] equipment."

"Number of targets with their coordinate measurement in TWS [Track While Scan] mode, pcs, 10."

"Number of simultaneously attacked targets", 1 [Su-30MKK] and 2 [Su-27SM(3)].

"Detection and tracking zone": ±60° in azimuth and -55° - +60° in elevation.

"Search and lock-on zone in close combat": ± 2° in azimuth and -10° to +50° in elevation.

"Detection range for an air target of a fighter type (RCS=3 m^2, with 0.5 probability)", look-up in forward hemisphere – no less than 100 km (in long range detection mode the range can be increased to 150 km); look-up in tail hemisphere – no less than 40 km; look-down in forward hemisphere – no less than 80 km; look-down in tail hemisphere – no less than 35 km.

"Operation range of RVV-AE radio correction channel: up to 40 km".

"In 'Air to Ground' mode the radar provides as follows: detection of ground and surface targets in real beam mapping mode, while scanning in low resolution mode (LRM), detection of ground and surface targets in SAR [Synthetic Aperture Radar] mapping mode in medium and high resolution modes (MRH, HRH), detection of ground and surface moving targets in ground moving target selection mode (GMTS), tracking and coordinate measurement for a ground target, output of target designations to X-31A, X-59MK, X-35E missile RHH."

"In GMTS mode the radar provides for the detection of moving targets with RCS [Radar Cross Section] of about 10 m^2 (a tank) and more, and radial velocity" at ranges of 15-90 km.

"Characteristics in 'Air to Ground' mode, limits of search zone size: mapping in Real Beam mode (RB) ± 45° (within ± 60° angles); in sea search mode (SS) ± 45° (within ± 60° angles); in Doppler beam sharpening (DBS) 30° within ± (10° …60°) angles; in HRH mode 5° within ± 30° …60°) angles."

"Detection range" is stated as "'350 km' for an aircraft carrier with an RCS of 50000 m^2, '250 km' for a Destroyer with a RCS of 10000 m^2, 'no less than 100 km' for a railway bridge with RCS of 2000 m^2, '50-70 km' for a missile boat with a RCS of 500 m^2 and '30 km' for a boat with a RCS of 50 m^2."

The Su-27SM(3)/SKM would be equipped with the OEPS-27MK (Item 31E-MK) Optical Electronic Sight System combining an OLS-27MK (Article 52Sh) with a laser illumination system; the OLS-27MK performing the functions of an Infrared Search and Track system, the sensor housing being offset to starboard ahead of the windscreen as seen on Su-27SM3 Red 56 (above) and in close up on the next page. KnAAPO/Sukhoi

As is the case with the Su-30MKK and Su-30MK2, the Su-27SM/SKM are equipped with an OEPS-27MK (Item 31E-MK) Optical Electronic Sight System which combines an IRST (Infrared Search and Track) and laser illumination channel capability developed by the UMAZ (Urals Opto-mechanical plant). The Optical Location Station element of the system consists of the OLS-27MK (Article 52Sh) which provides the host aircraft with a passive (radar silent – non emitting radar emissions) detection, tracking and engagement capability, reducing overall vulnerability to enemy direct and indirect detection, tracking and engagement systems and countermeasures; such systems also proving to be effective at countering stealth technology.

The OLS, which can also be employed in conjunction with the radar, with which it is completely integrated, features an in azimuth tracking zone of ±- 60° and -15 to +60° in elevation. This system features a 60° in azimuth and 10° in elevation field of view and search; a 20° in azimuth and 5° in elevation small field of view and search; close combat area ('Vertical' mode) 3 x (-15° to + 60°; Lock-on area 3° x 3°.

Manufacturer information shows that the OLS-27MK system has a detection range against an air target in infrared contrast in the tail on aspect for a target in the class of a Sukhoi Su-15 interceptor operating without afterburner "(PMFU)" of "no less than 30 km". A target in the class of the RAC MiG-25 at high altitude in the forward aspect in afterburner at speeds of at least Mach 2.0 can be detected at "no less than 90 km". Against an airborne target in the RAC MiG-21 class the laser rangefinder can be operated at ranges up to "8 km" and 0.3 to 10 km against ground targets.

As is the case with the Su-30MKK/MK2/M2 family of two-seat multirole strike fighters the Su-27SM and Su-27SKM are equipped with a SILS-27M HUD (Heads up Display) which dominates the forward view from the cockpit, as seen on this Su-27SM3. KnAAPO

The other elements of the Weapons Control System, as noted above, consists of the SILS-27M HUD (Heads up Display), 6231R-9-2 IFF interrogator and the SURA-K HMTDS, which can scan the airspace ± 60° in azimuth and -20 to +60° in elevation (conflicting manufacturer documentations states that the scanning parameters are ± 70° in azimuth and -35° to +65° in elevation, the same as those of the SURA equipping the Su-30MKI/MKM/MKI(A), with a designation accuracy (RMS error) of < 3 mrad. The entire system weighing 10 kg; the helmet mounted element weighting 0.39 kg.

The Su-27SM(3)/Su-27SKM are equipped with the SURA-K HMTDS, which, while being less advanced than the SURA-M equipping some other Russian tactical combat aircraft such as the Su-30SM, remains a highly capable system employed by a number of air forces worldwide.

In simplified terms the HMTDS, which receives signal inputs from the various on-board systems, displays flight and targeting information on a visor on the pilot flight helmet. This data, which is displayed in symbolic and alphanumeric form, with various data types and volumes specified by individual operators, is projected on a field of view of 6° x 4°.

The WCS was designed with growth potential allowing the integration of the other weapons like the R-27P1(EP1) passive radiation homing air to air missile and new generation air to air and air to surface weapons – RVV-MD close-range infrared guided, and RVV-SD active-radar homing medium range air to air missiles and precision guided bombs with satellite guidance, KAB-500C-E (KAB-500S-E).

In the Su-27SM aircraft the pilot is seated on a NPP Zvezda K-36D zero-zero ejection seat, the pilot separating from the seat after the ejection process has propelled him/her clear of the aircraft. The seat provides the ability for safe ejection from a stricken aircraft at equivalent airspeeds of (V_E) 0 to 1300 km/h, with the capability to eject at Mach numbers up to 2.5 at any altitude from 0 to 20000 m even when the aircraft is a 0 airspeed and 0 altitude.

The cockpit layout in the Su-27SKM demonstrator Black 305 is dominated by the HUD, two colour MFDS and the colour multifunction panel. This is representative of the Su-27SM, but the Su-27SM3 is stated to feature four multifunction displays, this of course may be taking the HUD into consideration. Sukhoi

The partial glass cockpit of the Su-27SKM, although appearing outdated by $4^{th}++$ or $5^{th}+$ generation standards, is a generation ahead of the cockpit standard of the Su-27S/SK. The cockpit, which is dominated by the SILS-27M HUD (Heads Up Display) in front of the windscreen (this being integrated with a Berkt-1 video recording unit), apparently featured an open architecture avionics suite developed by RPKB Ramenskoye Design Bureau, which apparently included an SUV-P-E cockpit & fire control management system which incorporated a BTsVM-486-2M, or equivalent, computer and two 152 mm x 208 mm class MFI-10-6M colour MFDS (Multi-Function Display Screen) and a MFPI-6 colour multifunctional display panel featuring a number of push buttons. The displays can replicate all relevant targeting, weapons, fuel, flight and navigational data, these forming the major elements of the cockpit data management system, a number of traditional dial style cockpit controls being retained, most of which are for back-up purposes only. Other systems include the secure radio UHF and VHF communications system, compatible with modern ground based aerial communications system such as the NKVS-27 system, and a satellite navigation system, apparently an A-737-010, that is compatible with the Russian GLONASS and American NAVSTAR systems. The Su-27SM, the Su-27SM3 in particular, may at a later date be equipped with a variation of the BINS-SP-2 strap down inertial navigation system which would allow the aircraft to fly accurate navigation even in the absence of GPS signals, ground based or offshore navigational data.

The self-defence suite includes an L-150 Pastel RWR (Radar Warning Receiver) ELINT (Electronic Intelligence) system that, as well as alerting the pilot to threat radar systems, provides targeting information to the Kh-31P anti-radiation missiles in the defence suppression role. In its primary function the system provides the pilot with a detection (including in track-while scan mode) and direction finding capability and can prioritise threat radars providing the pilot with relative information on which systems pose the most immediate threat, an audible alarm sounding when the host aircraft has been illuminated by a threat radar from an aircraft or the seeker head of a semi-active or active radar guided missile, the radiation emissions of which are detected when the systems are actively operating in target acquisition, tracking and illumination mode. The system, which weighs 45 kg (excluding the display), operates in the 2-18 GHz frequency bands against quasi-continuous, continuous and pulse radar signals with a location accuracy of 3-10°.

The suite also includes decoy systems; UV-30MK chaff dispenser, which, as stated by JSC Tactical Missiles Corporation, jam "guidance systems and executive mechanisms with passive countermeasures effective in optical and radar frequency bands," and flare dispensers.

At the time of writing there is no evidence of wingtip mounted ECM systems, such as the Khbiny-U system carried by the and Su-30SM, being employed by the Su-27SM, although it is understood that less capable systems such as the Sorbtsiya ECM pods are amiable for the export Su-27SKM and an export variant of the Khbiny systems is under development.

Ordered for the Russian Federation Air Force at the same time as forty eight Su-35S 4th++ generation multidimensional fighter aircraft and four Su-30M2 multirole strike fighters, all of the twelve Su-27SM3 aircraft had been delivered by the end of 2011; the last example having been delivered to the Russian Federation Air Force towards the end of December that year. This new build variant introduced a host of improvements over the Su-27S(II), including a strengthened structure to enable take-off weights some 3 tons higher than that of the Su-27S. The powerplant was the uprated MMPP Salut AL-31F-M1 introduced on the second contract for upgrades of the Su-27S to Su-27SM standard. The avionics and fire control system was along the lines of those introduced on the Su-27SM, although some systems apparently featured enhancements over those installed in the upgraded aircraft. The glass cockpit featured an improved data control systems – four multifunctional displays completely replacing the first generation multi-dial ergonomics. A new improved communication system allows secure communications with other aircraft and ground control stations in a high threat jamming environment, other elements of the suite including a CIS integrated information system and enhanced ECM equipment.

The ten external stations of the Su-27S/SK/SM/SKM was increased to twelve on the Su-27SM3 for the carriage of air to air and air to surface stores including the addition of the ability employ new generation satellite guided bombs.

Top: Elements of the threat warning suite are located on the trailing edges of the vertical tails as shown on this Su-27SM3. Above: A Su-27SM3, with spine mounted airbrake deployed, is towed to dispersal in November 2011. KnAAPO

| Smart coupling units providing for linking between avionics and weapon | Integrated controller of autonomous operation (IKAR) | Peripheral coupling units providing for linking between avionics and weapon |

The Su-27SM/SKM avionics to weapons interface is based on the system developed for the Su-30MKK/MK2. Aviaavmatika

The Su-27SM/SKM variants can be armed with a wide diversity of radar and infrared homing air to air missiles and guided and unguided air to surface munitions, respective weapons being launched by data supplied via an armament management system developed by Aviaavmatika, this apparently being an SUO-30PKR-E unit.

It is of note that KnAAPO documentation and info-graphics show various munitions being carried on ten stations which is representative of the Su-27SM/SKM, the innermost wing stations available on such designs as the Su-30MK2 being absent. The technical reference to the Su-27SM (contracts for SM1 and SM2 aircraft upgraded from Su-27S) and the Su-27SKM clearly shows ten stations, this being the number of stations available on the first generation Su-27S. However, KnAAPO documentation refers to the number of stations available on the new build Su-27SM3 aircraft, which have a 3000 kg higher maximum take-off weight compared to the Su-27SM1/2/SKM, as being twelve. The weapons options and numbers outlined below are taken from KnAAPO documentation which omits the inner wing station usage that is available on the Su-27SM3, therefore, an open mind should be kept in regards to absolute number of weapons that could be carried by this variant, which would still be capable of carrying up to ten air to air missiles – six R-27 or RVV-AE and 4 R-73E, but, with the inner wing stations employed, additional air to surface stores could be carried, although it is unclear if such weapons as the Kh-59MK or Kh-59ME missiles may be integrated on the Su-27SM3; four and two of these weapons respectively ale to be carried.

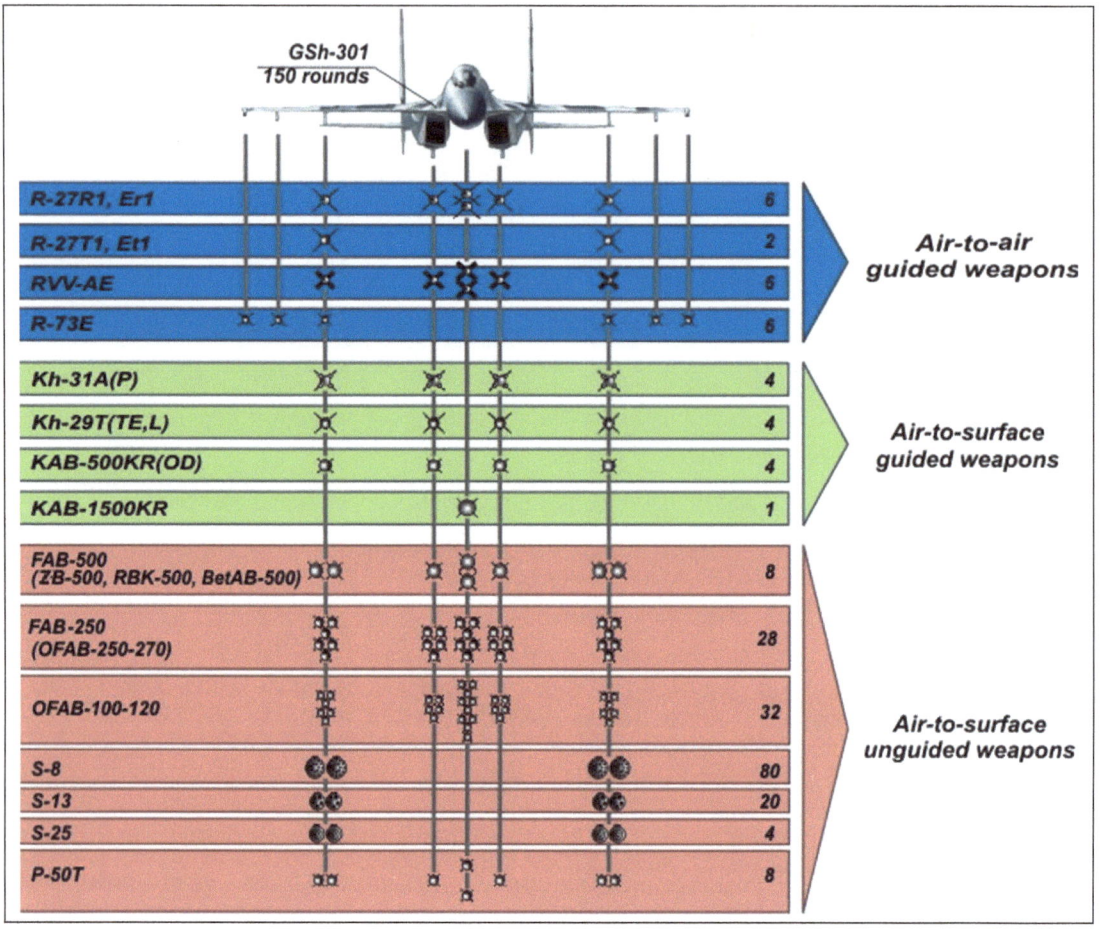

Chart depicting the standard air to air and air to surface weapons load out for the Su-27SKM which can be carried on ten stations, six wing, two engine trunk and two centre fuselage stations. In the Su-27SM3 variant, stores can be carried on twelve stations, two additional stations being activated on the inner wing sections, leading to what would be the inner wing stations on Su-27SM/SKM now being the inner intermediate stations on the Su-27SM3. In the air to surface mission the aircraft can operate with a mix of guided and unguided air to surface stores. In the air to air role the Su-27SM(3)/SKM variants can engage targets with active radar guided RVV-AE, semi-active-radar guided R-27R1(ER1) and infrared guided R-27T1(ET1) medium range missiles, as well as the highly agile R-73E infrared guided short-range air to air missile. Sukhoi

In addition to externally carried ordnance all variants are armed with an internal GSh-301 30 mm cannon found in other members of the extended Su-27 family. This powerful weapon, housed in the starboard wing-root with 150 round of ammunition, can fire at a rate of between 1,500 and 1,800 rounds per minute, with a muzzle velocity of 870 meters per second. The cannon has a range out to around 1800 meters in the air to air role or up to 800 meters against surface targets. For air to air and air to ground missions the cannon is primarily a secondary weapon.

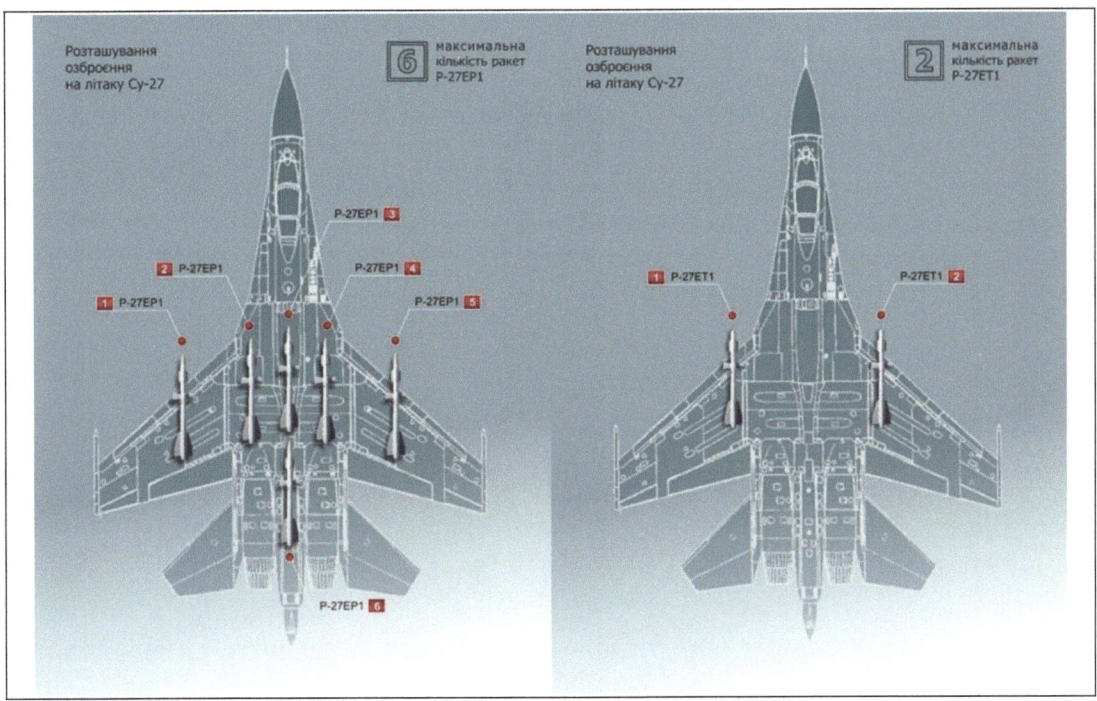

The graphic on the left depicts the maximum carriage of six R-27ER1 semi-active radar homing medium range air to air missile (the graphic states EP1, but this actually corresponds to the ER1). The graphic on the right shows the maximum carriage of two R-27ET1 infrared guided medium range air to air missile, which appears to be shown carried on the innermost wing section which would be unavailable on the Su-27SM/SKM, the ET1 missiles being carried on the innermost of the three stations available on each wing of this variant. Artem

The main driving force behind the Su-27SM/SKM updates were aimed at improving the designs multirole capabilities, particularly in regards to the carriage and employment of precision guided air to surface munitions. However, the designs primary operational role remained that of an air superiority fighter aircraft armed with the standard Russian medium and short-range air to air weapons; the Vympel (JSC Tactical Missiles Corporation) R-27R1(ER1), R-27T1(ET1), RVV-AE and R-73E (in Russian language the weapons are P-27, P-73 or K-27, K-73) a maximum mix of ten could be carried by the Su-27SM/SKM.

Entering service in the mid-1980's as the primary air to air armament of the Su-27S and MiG-29, the R-27 medium-range missile variants in service in 2016 are more capable updates of the R-27, of which a whole family of variants was produced, including the R-27R1, NATO reporting name AA-10 'Alamo' A with SARH (Semi-Active Radar Homing) guidance and the R-27T1 'Alamo' B with IR guidance. Longer range variants were also developed, designated R-27ER1 for the SARH variant and R-27ET1 for the passive infrared homing variant. These missiles, 'Alamo' C and 'Alamo' D respectively, are fitted with a boost sustain motor to extend engagement range.

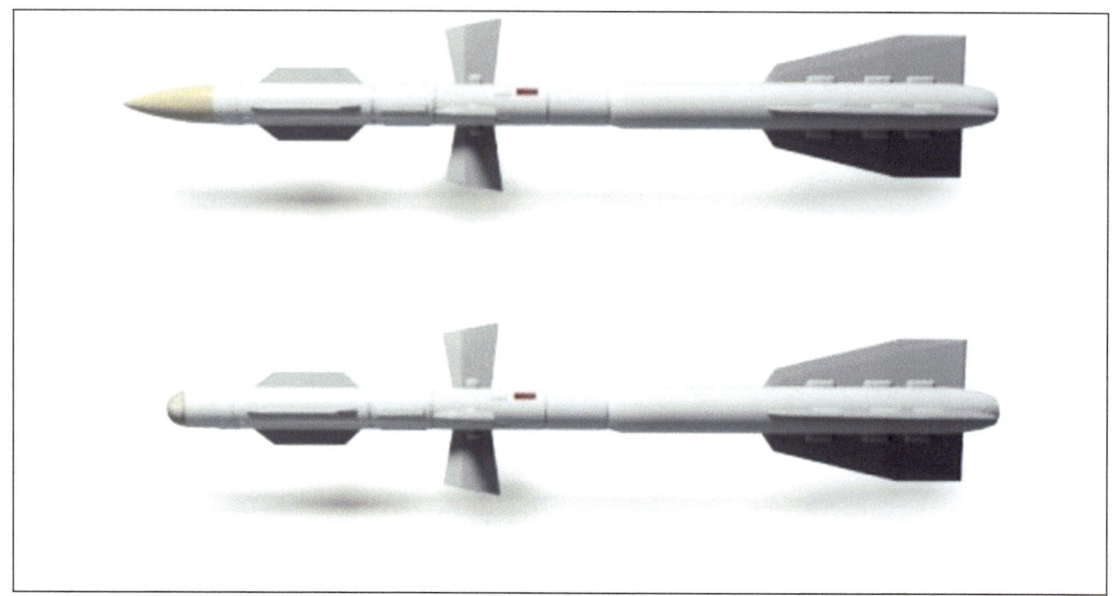

R-27ER1 semi-active radar homing medium range air to air missile (top) and R-27ET1 passive infrared guided medium range air to air missile (above). The R-27ER1 configuration is also representative of the R-27EP1. Artem

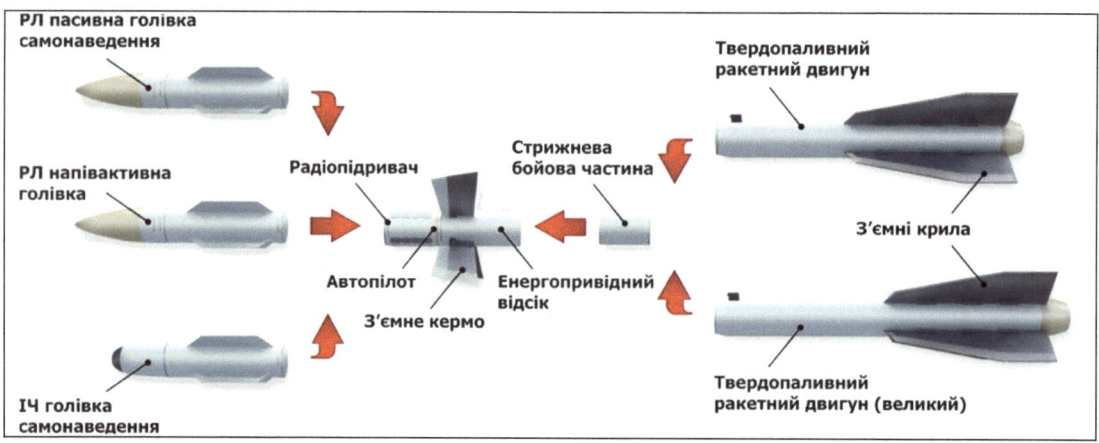

Ukrainian/Russo language graphic depicting a breakdown of the R-27 variants showing the seeker heads at left, semi-active radar homing, passive radiation homing and passive infrared homing, the central section consisting of the radio fuse, autopilot emergency devices unit and differential control fins followed by the rod type warhead and the tail sections at right, with the solid-propellant rocket motor for the R1/T1/P1 (top) and the tail module with the extended solid-propellant rocket motor for the ER1/ET1/EP1 (bottom). Artem

Up to six R-27R1(ER1) missiles can be carried by the Su-27SM/SKM – two on the centre fuselage stations, two on the engine trunk stations and one on each of the inner (inner intermediate on Su-27SM3) wing stations. Two R-27T1(ET1) can be carried on the inner wing stations in place of two of the R-27R1(ER1) missiles.

The R-27ER1 is arguably the best weapon in its class. Despite its reliance on semi-active radar homing technology, which requires the carrier aircraft to continuously illuminate the target during the missile flight, remaining a highly capable radar guided air to air missile even in the age of active radar guided missile proliferation. Author

The R-27ER1 has a length of 4.775 m, diameter 0.26 m at solid rocket motor section and 0.23 m at control unit section, wing span of 0.803 m and control plane span of 0.972 m. The R-27ET1 dimensions are the same as those of the R-27ER1 with the exception of length which is slightly reduced at 4.49 m. The R-27ER1 has a launch weight of 350 kg whilst the R-27ET1 launch weight, at 343 kg, is slightly lower. Missile flight speed is Mach 4, the R-27ER1 having an engagement range of 60 to 62.5 km against a fighter aircraft size target and up to 100 km when used against larger targets such as an AWACS (Airborne Warning and Control System) platform. The infrared guided R-27ET1 has an engagement range of 80 km against a target in the front hemisphere. Both variants are armed with a 39 kg expanding rod warhead.

Complementing the infrared guided R-27T1(ET1) is the smaller, shorter range, highly agile, Vympel (JSC Tactical Missiles Corporation) R-73E infrared homing missile, six of which can be carried, one on each of the inner, intermediate (inner and outer intermediate on Su-27SM3) and outer wing stations. The R-73E was a generation ahead of its rivals when it entered service in the 1980's, comparable systems being fielded by NATO air arms only in the first decade of the 21st century.

In 2016, the R-73E remains the standard short-range air to air missile in Russian Federation Air Force service. Author

The R-73 was developed with high agility as a design driver, augmented by the ability of the pilot of the host aircraft, be it an Su-27 or derivative or a MiG-29 or derivative, to cue the weapon to targets at up to 60° off-boresight via a HPS (Helmet Pointing System) or the 21st century HMTDS (Helmet Mounted Target Designation System), a SURA-K system in the Su-27SM/SKM. High manoeuvrability was achieved by a combination of a number of factors, including four forward control fins, elevators attached to the rear fins, which are fixed, and deflector vanes positioned in the nozzle of the rocket engine.

The R-73E has a length of 2.9 m, diameter 0.17 m, wing span 0.51 m and control plane span of 0.38 m, launch weight being 105 kg. The missile, which has a longer reach than most western equivalents, has a maximum engagement range of 30 km against a head-on target and a minimum engagement range of 0.3 km against a tail-on target manoeuvring at up to 12 g. The missile can be launched at altitudes from 0.02 km up to 20 km, the all-aspect passive infrared seeker head guiding the missile to the target, which would then be destroyed by the 8 kg expanding rod warhead.

Up to six RVV-AE active radar guided medium range air to air missiles can be carried by the Su-27SM/SKM, one on each of the inner wing stations (inner intermediate on the Su-27SM3), one on each of the engine trunk stations and two carried in tandem on the centre fuselage stations.

Development of this weapon apparently commenced in 1982 and the missile entered limited service in the mid-1990's, certainly with trials units in Russia. Into the 21st century the weapon has been integrated onto a number of aircraft types undergoing updates as well as new aircraft of the Su-27SM3, Su-30, Su-34, Su-35S, and MiG-29 variants, as well as the Sukhoi T-50 PAK FA fifth generation multirole fighter aircraft. The weapon has also been exported to a number of customers.

The RVV-AE has a length of 3.6 m, diameter 0.2 m, wingspan 0.4 m, control plane span 0.7 m and a launch weight of 175 kg, has narrow-span wings of rectangular shape and four lattice control surfaces at the rear. Operational parameters include a minimum engagement range of 0.3 km in the rear hemisphere and a maximum range of 80 km in the forward hemisphere, the missile reaching speeds of Mach 4 and able to engage targets manoeuvring at up to 12 g from 0.2 to 25 km altitude.

An RVV-AE is launched from what appears to be a Su-27UB two seat operational conversion trainer aircraft, several of which serve with each of the Regiments equipped with Su-27SM's.

Like its western rivals, the US Raytheon AIM-120A/C AMRAAM (Advanced Medium Range Air to Air Missile) and the European MICA EM, the RVV-AE can be employed in a launch-and-forget mode and features a multi-stage guidance system that includes inertial command in the initial phase with mid-course updates via an aircraft to missile datalink for long-range engagements, with active radar homing in the terminal phase of the engagement; the on-board active-radar apparently having an acquisition-range of around 20 km. The missile, which features an active-radar fuse for the 22.5 kg warhead, can apparently be used in a 'self-defence' mode to intercept missiles launched at the mother aircraft, although how effective this capability is, or if indeed such a capability is viable for the technology involved, is unclear. The designer noted that whilst the RVV-AE is heavier than the AIM-120A/C and MICA EM, the Russian missile has a longer range and better performance when engaging manoeuvring targets compared to its western rivals.

The Su-27SKM demonstrator, Black 305, is shown with all ten stores stations occupied; four x R-73E air to air missiles carried on the outer and intermediate wing stations, two RVV-AE air to air missiles carried on the inner wing stations, two R-27ER1 air to air missiles carried in tandem on the centre fuselage stations and two Kh-31P anti-radiation missiles carried on the engine trunk stations. UAC

The Su-27SKM/SM can be armed with the JSC Tactical Missiles Corporation Kh-31A anti-ship missile and the Kh-31P anti-radiation missile, a total of four of any one variant or a mix of both variants able to be accommodated; the missiles being carried one on each of the inner (inner intermediate on the Su-27SM3) wing stations and one on each of the engine trunk stations. The Kh-31P is cleared on the domestic Su-27SM (apparently since November 2008), but there is a lack of clarity as to whether or not the Kh-31A has been cleared for use on the Su-27SM(3).

The Kh-31P, which is designed to engage continuous-wave and pulsed radar systems of the type found in modern medium and long range air defence systems, is carried on and launched from an AKU-58 airborne ejection unit. Targeting data can be handed down to the missile from the carrier aircraft sensors prior to launch or the homing head can autonomously search for and lock-on to a target.

The Kh-31P, which has a launch weight of around 600 kg, has a length of 4.7 m, a diameter of 0.36 m and a wing span of 0.914 m, can be launched from altitudes of 100 m to 15000 m at a carrier speed of Mach 0.65 to Mach 1.25, after which it flies to targets between 15 to 110 km away (depending upon launch altitude) at speeds of 1000 m/s (3600 km/h). The target is destroyed by an 87 kg high explosive fragmentation warhead.

Su-27SKM Black 305 shown with four R-73E air to air missiles on the outer and intermediate wing stations, two R-27ER1 air to air missiles in tandem on the fuselage centre stations (one of which is obscured by the starboard engine trunk), two Kh-31P anti-radiation missiles on the engine trunk stations and two Kh-29 short-range air to surface missiles on the inner wing stations. Sukhoi

Up to four of the Kh-31A anti-ship missile, which has the same overall dimensions, similar launch weight, and identical launch parameters to the Kh-31P, can be carried and launched from an AKU-58A ejection unit on the same stations as the latter missile. The on-board active-radar homing head of the Kh-31A can designate targets in both pre-and-post launch modes and conduct target acquisition and selection, and, as stated in JSC Tactical Missiles Corporation documentation, determines "target coordinates (range, azimuth, elevation), generation of command signals", which are fed directly to the guidance system, the missiles being launched either singly or in salvo in clear and adverse weather conditions in a high threat active jamming environment. Once launched the missile cruises at a speed of 1000 m/s to targets 5 to 70 km distant (against a Destroyer size target) depending on launch altitude, the target being destroyed or disabled by the 95 kg warhead.

As is the case with most Russian tactical combat aircraft the standard battlefield air to surface missiles integrated on the Su-27SM/SKM is the Kh-29TE(L) family of short range air to surface weapons, four of which can be carried on the same stations as used for the carriage of the Kh-31A/P. Designed for use against hardened targets such as large bridges, reinforced runways, industrial centres and hardened aircraft shelters, the Kh-29 family can also be employed effectively against surface vessels with a displacement up to 10,000 tons.

The Kh-29 missiles, which are 3.9 m in length, 0.4 m diameter, 1.1 m wing span and have a launch weight of 690 kg for the Kh-29TE and 660 kg for the Kh-29L, are carried on and launched from AKU-58AE airborne ejector units; the Kh-29TE being guided to the target by a passive TV (Television) guidance system whilst the Kh-29L is fitted with a semi-active laser guidance system; the target being destroyed by the 320 kg high explosive penetrating warhead. JSC Tactical Missiles Corporation documentation shows the missile to have a minimum engagement range of 3 km and a maximum engagement range of 20 to 30 km for the Kh-29TE (depending on launch altitude) and 10 km for the Kh-29L

As well as guided air to surface missiles, the Su-27SM/SKM family are cleared to operate with KAB-500Kr(OD) and KAB-1500Kr guided bomb units, four of the 520 kg weight KAB-500Kr or four of the 370 kg KAB-500OD weapons able to be carried on the same stations as employed for the Kh-31/Kh-29 missiles, but only one of the larger 1525 kg weight KAB-1500Kr weapons able to be carried between the fuselage centre stations. The higher maximum take-off weight and two additional wing stations on the Su-27SM3 would enable this variant to operate with up to six KAB-500 or three KAB-1500 weapons as is the case with the Su-30MK2/M2.

The KAB-500 weapons, which are 3.05 m in length with a 0.35 m diameter and can be released from altitudes of 0.5 to 5 km at carrier speeds of 550 to 1100 km/h, have a root mean square deviation of 4-7 m, the target being destroyed by the 380 kg concrete piercing high explosive penetrator warhead in the KAB-500Kr or the 250 kg high explosive fuel air warhead in the KAB-500OD.

Launch parameters for the KAB-1500Kr are 1 to 8 km altitude and 550 to 1100 km/h carrier speed, with a root mean square deviation of 4-7 m, the target being destroyed by the 1170 kg high explosive penetrating warhead.

Previous page and above: Su-27SKM demonstrator Black 05 deploys KAB-500 guided bomb units. Sukhoi

As well as the weapons specified, the Su-27SM/SKM can have other weapons integrated such as the Kh-38 family of battlefield tactical missiles, Kh-35E anti-ship missiles and guided bomb units such as the LFB-250 smart bomb unit. The Kh-59MK long-range air to surface stand-off missile, is apparently not cleared on the Su-27SM/SKM, but could be carried, one on each of the inner wing stations of the Su-27SM3 and possibly two more on the inner intermediate wing stations in the same fashion to that seen on the Su-30MK2/M2 which can operate with four such weapons.

Enhancements to the air to air armament would be possible with integration of the RVV-MD and RVV-SD new generation of infrared guided and active radar guided air to air missiles developed as replacement for the R-73E and RVV-AE respectively.

The Su-27SM/SKM family can also employ a range of unguided munitions including FAB-500 (ZB-500, RBK-500, BetAB-500) general purpose bombs, up to eight of which can be carried; two on each of the inner wing stations, two on fuselage centre station and one on each of the intake stations. Twenty eight of the smaller FAB-250 (OFAB-250-270) general purpose bombs can be carried in clusters on the same stations as used for the FAB-500 series. Alternatively the same stations can be used to carry up to thirty two OFAB-100-120 general purpose bombs.

Unguided rockets can include up to four B-8M-1 rocket pods; two on each of the inner wing stations (holding a combined total of 80 rockets) or four smaller B-13L rocket pods (holding a combined total of 20 rockets) can be carried on the same stations. An alternative is four S-25, S-25OOFM-PU rockets which are carried on the same stations as the B-8M-1 and B-13L. KnAAPO documentation shows that up to eight of the P-50T weapons can be carried on the inner wing stations (two each), fuselage centre station and engine intake stations.

Page 46-48: Su-27SKM demonstrator Black 305 flight demonstrations with a range of air to air and air to surface guided weapons. Sukhoi/KnAAPO

3

OPERATIONAL AIRCRAFT AND UNITS

The Russian Federation Air Force had formulated plans for various upgrade programs for elements of its various tactical combat aircraft fleets in 1999, this being refined before being approved by President Putin in 2002. In regards to its Su-27S air superiority fighter fleet, the upgrade that was formulated corresponded to building on development work carried out for the avionics and fire control systems developed for the Su-30MK2 two-seat multirole strike fighter developed for the export market, China being the major customer.

To flight test the upgrade configuration the Russian Federation Air Force provided an Su-27S with the serial code 38-02 and the side code Red 56, which was taken direct from the resident 23rd IAP (Fighter Aircraft Regiment) at Dzemgi air base, which was co-operated by KnAAPO (Komsomolsk-on-Amur Aircraft Production Association). This aircraft was modified to the first baseline Su-27SM standard, this being complete by late 2002, the aircraft being flown in Su-27SM configuration by Sukhoi test pilot Yevgeny Frolov on 27 December that year. A short series of test flights was then conducted from Komsomolsk-on-Amur and Zhukovsky before the aircraft was transferred to Akhtubinsk to embark upon a trials program. A further aircraft, formerly the Su-30KI, serial code 40-02, was modified for incorporation into the test program for which it received the Su-27SKM designation with the Bort code Black 305, indicating that it was the export configuration of the domestic Su-27SM.

In 2003, Sukhoi was contracted to upgrade 24 Su-27S to Su-27SM standard at JSC KnAAPO, Komsomolsk-on-Amur, as the Russian Federation Air Force embarked upon implementation of the plans to enhance the capability of its ageing fleet of combat aircraft. The first Su-27SM's, a batch of five aircraft, apparently Red 02, 03, 04, 05 and 07, were handed over to the Russian Federation Air Force on 26 December 2003, following which they were transferred to the CCTC (Combat Conversion Training Centre) at Lipetsk where pilots and ground personnel were trained in operation of the aircraft enhanced capabilities. In 2004, the Su-27SM was recommended for operational service leading to conversion of pilots and ground personnel from an operational unit, the 23rd IAP, seven aircraft being handed over to the unit at Dzemgi in a ceremony at Komsomolsk-on-Amur on 23 December that year. Around eleven additional Su-27SM's were delivered in 2005, followed by the balance of six, of the initial contract for 24 conversions, in November 2006, completing the three year contract allowing the complete re-equipment of the recipient Regiment. At this time a second contract covering upgrade of another 24 Su-27S to Su-27SM standard was being finalised as part of the Russian drive to modernise its air arms, which included modernisation of other aircraft types, including the Su-24M strike aircraft, and pushing ahead with plans to introduce new $4^{th}+/4^{th}++$ and fifth generation combat aircraft commencing with the Su-34 strike aircraft.

Acceptance ceremony for the first batch of Su-27SM's delivered to the Russian Federation Air Force 23nd IAP in December 2004. Sukhoi

The 22nd GvIAP (Guards Aviation Fighter Regiment) of the 11th Air Army, based at Centralnya Uglovava in the Russian Far East, was selected as the second regiment for re-equipment with the Su-27SM, the first aircraft from the second contract being delivered to this unit in December 2007, with the last of the 24 aircraft covered by the contract being delivered by Sukhoi to the unit on 23 September 2009, bringing to 48 the number of Su-27's upgraded under the modernisation program.

As noted above, the second contract for 24 upgraded aircraft incorporated the AL-31F-M1 (Series 42 M1) engine which provided improved performance, including a higher maximum thrust rating. It appears that at least some of the Su-27SM's converted under the first contract received AL-31F-M1 engines as they were taken in for overhaul or maintenance.

Top: Su-27SM Red 73, one of the aircraft covered under the first modernisation contract. KnAAPO **Above: Su-27SM's Red 76 and Red 92 from the first modernisation contract.** Rostec Corporation

Top: Su-27SM, Red 76, operating from Petropavlovsk-Kamchatski, intercepts a simulated hijacked airliner on 7 August 2011 during a joint US-Russian exercise. Above: Su-27SM's Blue 21 and Blue 33, both aircraft covered under the second modernisation contract, in company with an Su-27UB, Blue 40, intercept a simulated hijacked airliner during the joint US-Russian exercise Vigilant Eagle 13 on 27 August 2013; the exercise being administered from Joint Base Elmendorf-Richardson, Alaska. USAF

Sukhoi Su-27SM(3)/SKM

Sukhoi Su-27SM(3)/SKM

Sukhoi Su-27SM(3)/SKM

Sukhoi Su-27SM(3)/SKM

Page 53-67: Russian Federation Air Force Su-27SM3 air and ground operations on 26 November 2011. KnAAPO

Under a contract signed between the Ministry of Defence of the Russian Federation and Sukhoi, twelve new build Su-27SM3 multirole fighters were ordered in August 2009 at the same time as forty eight of the more advanced 4th++ generation Su-35S multidimensional fighter aircraft and four Su-30M2 multirole strike fighters, the latter equipped with much of the same systems as the Su-27SM, the new aircraft to be built at KnAAPO.

The first four Su-27SM3's, Red 51 (RF-93729), Red 52, Red 53 (RF-93730) and Red 54 (RF-93731), were apparently delivered to the 3rd IAP at Krimsk (Krymsk), Kondor Region, in February 2011, and the balance of eight, with codes Red 55, 56, 57, 58, 59, 60, 61 and 62, had been delivered to the Russian Federation Air Force by late December that year, bringing to 60 the number of Su-27SM/SM3 aircraft delivered to the Russian Federation Air Force.

In recent years the Russian air arms have undergone a number of administrative reorganisations including the introduction of the Air Base organisational system under which the 22nd GvIAP at Centralnava Uglovana was incorporated into the command structure of the 6987th Air Base and the 23rd IAP came under the structure of the 6989th Air Base.

The 22nd GvIAP and 23rd IAP are apparently to convert completely to the Su-35S, although the status of any such conversion is unclear in early 2016 as is the disposition of any Su-27SM's that may be transferred to other units.

The Indonesian TNI AU (Tentara Nasional Indonesia Angkatan Udara) operates three Su-27SKM multirole fighters, including TS-2703 (above) in a mixed force including small numbers of two-seat Su-30MK2 multirole strike fighters and Su-27SK air superiority fighters with a secondary air to surface capability. Commonwealth of Australia

To date the Su-27SKM has met with little success in regards to orders, a handful of such aircraft being delivered to Indonesia. Although the planned purchase of the single-seat Su-30KI, progenitor to the Su-27SKM, did not materialise due to financial constraints, Indonesia retained its requirement for modern fighter aircraft leading, as mentioned above, to small scale purchases of Su-27 derivatives from 2002. The numbers of aircraft purchased constituted only a token force of two Su-27SK and two Su-30MK2's, the former being delivered as air freight on 27 August 2002, followed by delivery of the two Su-30MK2's on 1 September 2003. Indonesian planned, in the longer term, to increase the number of Su-27/30's to between 12 and 16 airframes, which would allow equipment of a full operational squadron mix of Su-27SK and Su-30MK2's. To this end, in late 2003, it was announced that Indonesia hoped to purchase a further six Su-27SK and a pair of Su-30MK2's, a contract being signed on 23 July 2008 for the purchase of three Su-30MK2's and three of the enhanced Su-27SKM single-seat fighters, two of the Su-30MK2's arriving in Indonesia from KnAAPO on 29 December that year, the third arriving on 17 January 2009.

The three Su-27SKM fighters were delivered in September 2010; two being flown from KnAAPO to Sultan Hasanuddin air base, where they arrived on the 10th of the month, followed by the third which was delivered by an Antonov An-124 transport aircraft on the 16th of the month. These six new fighter aircraft, together with the older Su-27SK and Su-30MK2's purchased in 2003, would form an understrength operational Squadron.

Sukhoi Su-27SM(3)/SKM

Page 69-76: Russian Federation Air Force Su-27SM3 operations on 22 December 2011. KnAAPO

The Su-27SM/SKM configuration, with its updated avionics and systems, vastly enhanced the air to air and air to surface capabilities, in the former the addition of the RVV-AE provided a quantum leap in medium range air to air capability while in the latter the addition of precision guided munitions such as the Kh-29TE/L, Kh-31A/P and KAB-500Kr/1500Kr, allow the engagement of a multitude of ground and sea surface targets. When assessing the effectiveness of the new build Su-27SM3, Sukhoi stated that the design was "2 times as efficient [as] …its predecessor" when deployed against air targets and 3 times more capable against ground targets.

Although less advanced than the current stable of advanced fighters coming out of Russia, the Su-30SM, Su-35S, MiG-35/D and the fifth generation Sukhoi T-50 PAK FA, the introduction of the Su-27SM(3) allowed the Russian Federation Air Force to retain a viable 4th+ generation fighter element as it awaited its new fleets of advanced fighter aircraft, the Su-30SM entering service in 2013, the Su-35S entering service in 2014 and deliveries of production standard T-50 PAK FA (*Perspektivniy Aviacionniy Complex Frontovoi Aviacii* – Perspective Aviation Complex for Front line Aviation) fifth generation fighter aircraft expected to commence in late 2016/early 2017 under 2016 planning.

APPENDICES

APPENDIX I

No detailed specification has been released for the Su-27SM, however, in most respects this would correspond to that of the Su-27S, although there will be slight differences in regards to operating weights and performance improvements may be more profound in such areas as increased acceleration and climb rates when the higher thrust and increased fuel performance of the AL-31F-M1 engine is taken into account.

The specification for the Su-27SM is based on that of the Su-27S/SK with additions relative to the Su-27SM when known or inferred. Sukhoi data

Powerplant: 2 x AL-31F-1M (Series 42) afterburning turbofan engines each rated at 13500 kgf maximum thrust
Length: 21.9 m
Wingspan: 14.7 m
Height: 5.9 m
Normal take-off weight: 23400 kg with 2 x R-27R1 and 2 x R-73E missiles and 5270 kg of fuel
Maximum take-off weight: 30450 kg
Maximum landing weight: 23000 kg
Maximum internal fuel load: 9400 kg
Maximum ordnance load: 4430 kg (this value corresponds to that of the Su-27S, but may have been increased, which would also result in increased maximum take-off weights, although, without structural strengthening this would be marginal)
Maximum speed at sea level: 1400 km/h in clean configuration
Maximum Mach number: 2.35 (this value is representative of the Su-27S)
Ceiling: 18.5 km in clean configuration
Operational range configured with 2 x R-27R1 and 2 x R-73E air to air missiles when the missiles are launched at "half distance": 1340 km at sea level and 3530 km at altitude
Take-off run: 450 m at normal take-off weight
Landing run with braking parachute: 620 m at normal landing weight
Load limit: 9 g
Crew: 1

APPENDIX II

Su-27SKM
Powerplant: 2 x AL-31F afterburning turbofan engines each rated at 12500 kgf -2% in afterburner and in excess of 7670 kgf in full military power ± 2%
Length: 21.9 m
Wingspan: 14.7 m
Height: 5.9 m
Maximum take-off weight: 33000 kg
Maximum internal fuel load: 9400 kg
In-flight refuelling system: 1100 l/m at "maximum flow rate (at entry pressure of 3.5 kg/cm^2)
Maximum payload: 8000 kg
Maximum speed at sea level: 1400 km/h in clean configuration
Maximum Mach number: 2.15
Ceiling: 17.75 km in clean configuration
Range at cruising altitude: 3530 km
Take-off run: 450 m at normal take-off weight
Landing run with braking parachute: 700 m
Load limit: 9 g
Crew: 1

APPENDIX III

Su-27SM3
Powerplant: 2 x AL-31F-1M (Series 42) afterburning turbofan engines each rated at 13500 kgf thrust
Length: 21.9 m
Wingspan: 14.7 m
Height: 5.9 m
Normal take-off weight: In excess of the Su-27S value of 23400 kg with 2 x R-27R1 and 2 x R-73E missiles and 5270 kg of fuel
Maximum take-off weight: ~33450 kg
Maximum internal fuel load: 9400 kg
Maximum payload: 8000 kg
Maximum speed at sea level: 1400 km in clean configuration
Maximum Mach number: ~2.25
Ceiling: ~18 km in clean configuration
Operational range: similar value to that of the Su-27SM
Take-off run: 450 m at normal take-off weight
Landing run with braking parachute: ~700 m at normal landing weight
Load limit: 9 g
Crew: 1

APPENDIX IV

Development aircraft			
Aircraft	Serial	Code	First Flight
Su-30KI	40-02	Black 27	28 June 1998
Su-27SM	38-02	Red 56	27 December 2002 (previously operated as a serial Su-27S)
Su-27SKM	40-02	Black 305	2003 (flew as the Su-30KI on 28 June 1998)

APPENDIX V

Su-27SM1 – Twenty four serial production Su-27S upgraded, under the first upgrade contract, to Su-27SM standard initially with standard overhauled AL-31F engines

Red 01, Red 02, Red 03, Red 04, Red 06, Red 07, Red 69, Red 70, Red 71, Red 72, Red 73, Red 74, Red 75, Red 76, Red 77, Red 78, Red 79, Red 80, Red 81, Red 82, Red 83, Red 84, Red 85, Red 86, Red 87, Red 88, Red 89, Red 90, Red 91, Red 92

Su-27SM2 - Twenty four serial production Su-27S upgraded, under the second upgrade contract, to Su-27SM standard powered by MMPP Salut AL-31F-M1 engines

Blue 01, Blue 02, Blue 03, Blue 04, Blue 05, Blue 06, Blue 07, Blue 08, Blue 09, Blue 10, Blue 11, Blue 12, Blue 20, Blue 21, Blue 22, Blue 23, Blue 24, Blue 25, Blue 26, Blue 27, Blue 28, Blue 29, Blue 30, Blue 31, Blue 32, Blue 38

Su-27SM3 – Twelve new built aircraft featuring a number of improvements including a 3 ton higher maximum take off weight

Red 51 (RF-93729), Red 52, Red 53 (RF-93730), Red 54 (RF-93731), Red 55, Red 56, Red 57, Red 58, Red 59, Red 60, Red 61 and Red 62

Note: In regards to the Su-27SM upgrades form the two contracts there are more than 24 reported codes from each contract, this, it being assumed due to either reallocation of codes or misreporting of a number of codes. In regards to the first upgrade contract it is possible that at least some of the first batch of codes starting with 01 were later removed as these aircraft were delivered to an operational unit, although Red 06 was certainly still in use in 2009. In regards to the codes allocated to the aircraft upgraded under the second contract the code Blue 38 may be a documentation misprint and should possibly read Blue 33.
Note 2: It is thought that at least two Su-27SM's have been lost in accidents, one from the 23rd IAP in January 2010 and one from the 22nd IAP in April 2011.

APPENDIX VI

Indonesian Su-27SK/SKM	
Variant	Serial
Su-27SK	TS-2701
Su-27SK	TS-2702
Su-27SKM	TS-2703
Su-27SKM	TS-2704
Su-27SKM	TS-2705

APPENDIX VII

Operating Unit	Location
CCTC (apparently the 4th TiSBP I PLS)	Lipetsk
23rd IAP	Dzemgi (co-operated by KnAAPO)
22nd GvIAP	Centralnaya Uglovaya
6987th Air Base	Centralnaya Uglovaya
6989th Air Base	Dzemgi
3rd IAP	Krimsk, Kondor Region (Su-27SM3)

GLOSSARY

ACS	Automatic Control System
AIM	Airborne Interception Missile
AMRAAM	Advanced Medium Range Air to Air Missile
ANG	Air National Guard
AoA	Angle of Attack
AWACS	Airborne Warning and Control System
CCTC	Combat Conversion Training Centre
Cobra	Extreme high angle of attack manoeuvre
DBS	Doppler Beam Sharpening
DME	Distance Measuring Equipment
ECM	Electronic Counter Measures
EDCS	Electronic Distance Control System
ELINT	Electronic Intelligence
EW	Electronic Warfare
F	Fighter
FADEC	Full Authority Digital Engine Control
FBW	Fly By Wire
FCS	Flight Control System
FX	Fighter Experimental
g	Gravity (1 g = 1 x Earth gravity)
G	Gravity (1 G = 1 x Earth gravity)
GFRI	Gromov Flight Research Institute
GLONASS	Globanaya Navigozionnaya Sputnikovaya Sistema (Global Navigation Satellite System)
GMTS	Ground Moving Target Selection
GPS	Global Positioning System
GvIAP	Guards Aviation Fighter Aircraft Regiment
HMTDS	Helmet Mounted Target Designation System
HP	High Pressure
HRH	High Resolution mode
HUD	Heads Up Display
IAP	Fighter Aircraft Regiment
IAPA	Irkut Aircraft production Association (now Irkut Corporation)
IA-PVO	*Istrebitelnaya Aviatsiya Protivo-Vozdushnoy Obstrany*/Air Defence Force
IFF	Identification Friend or Foe
IRST	Infra-Red Search and Track
ISIS	Islamic State (also referred to as ISIL and Daesh)
JSC	Joint Stock Company
kgf	Kilogram Force
kg/s	Kilograms per second

km	Kilometre
km/h	Kilometre per Hour
kN	Kilo Newton
KnAAPO	Komsomolsk-on-Amur Aircraft Production Association
LERX	Leading Edge Root Extension
l/m	Litre per Minute
LP	Low Pressure
LPC	Low Pressure Compressor
LRM	Low Resolution Mode
m	Metre
m²	Metre Squared
m/s	Metres per second
Mach	Speed of Sound
MFDS	Multi-Function Display Screen
MiG	Mikoyan
MKI	Modernised Commercial India
MKM	Modernised Commercial Malaysian
MODRF	Ministry of Defence of the Russian Federation
mrad	Milliradian - Unit of angular measurement (1000 mrad = 1 radian)
MRCA	Multi-Role Combat Aircraft
MRH	Medium Resolution mode
NATO	North Atlantic Treaty Organisation
NAVSTAR	Navigation Satellite Timing and Ranging System
OEPS	Optical Electronic Sighting System
OLS	Optical Location Station
PAK FA	*Perspektivniy Aviacionniy Complex Frontovoi Aviacii* – Perspective Aviation Complex for Front line Aviation
PFI	Advanced Frontline Fighter
PLAAF	Peoples Liberation Army Air Force
RB	Real Beam
RCS	Radar Cross Section
RHH	Radar Homing Head
RWR	Radar Warning Receiver
S	Serial
SAR	Synthetic Aperture Radar
SARH	Semi-Active Radar Homing
SM	Serial Modernised
SS	Sea Search
Su	Sukhoi
Tail Slide	Extreme high angle of attack manoeuvre
TNI AU	Tentara Nasional Indonesia Angkatan Udara
TV	Television
TWS	Track While Scan
UMAZ	Urals Opto-Mechanical Plant
US	United States

USAF	United States Air Force
V_E	Velocity
VOR	Very High Frequency Omnidirectional Range
WCS	Weapons Control System
x	Times (multiplication)
±	Plus or minus
<	Strict inequality – Less than
~	Approximately equal to (can also be used to mean asymptotically equal)
°	Degree

ABOUT THE AUTHOR

Hugh, a historian and author, with extensive studies in astrophysics, aeronautics and astronautics, has published in excess of sixty books; non-fiction and fiction, writing under his given name as well as utilising two different pseudonyms. He has also written for several international magazines, whilst his work has been used as reference for many other projects ranging from the aviation industry, international news corporations and film media to encyclopaedias, museum exhibits and the computer gaming industry. He currently resides in his native Scotland

Other titles by the author include

Sukhoi T-50/PAK FA - Russia's 5th Generation 'Stealth' Fighter
Sukhoi Su-35S 'Flanker' E - Russia's 4++ Generation Super-Manoeuvrability Fighter
Sukhoi Su-34 'Fullback'
Sukhoi Su-30MKK/MK2/M2 - Russo Kitashiy Striker from Amur
MiG-35/D 'Fulcrum' F – Towards the Fifth Generation
Air War over Syria, Tu-160, Tu-95MS & Tu-22M3 - Cruise Missile and Bombing Strikes on Syria, November 2015-February 2016
November 2015-February 2016
Eurofighter Typhoon - Storm over Europe
Tornado F.2/F.3 Air Defence Variant
Air to Air Missile Directory
North American F-108 Rapier - Mach 3 Interceptor
Convair YB-60 - Fort Worth Overcast
Boeing X-36 Tailless Agility Flight Research Aircraft
X-32 - The Boeing Joint Strike Fighter
X-35 - Progenitor to the F-35 Lightning II
X-45 Uninhabited Combat Air Vehicle
Into The Cauldron - The Lancaster MK.I Daylight Raid on Augsburg
Light Battle Cruisers and the Second Battle of Heligoland Bight
British Battlecruisers of World War 1 - Operational Log, July 1914-June 1915
Hurricane IIB Combat Log - 151 Wing RAF, North Russia 1941
RAF Meteor Jet Fighters in World War II, an Operational Log
Typhoon IA/B Combat Log - Operation Jubilee, August 1942
Defiant MK.I Combat Log - Fighter Command, May-September 1940
Blenheim MK.IF Combat Log - Fighter Command Day Fighter Sweeps/Night Interceptions, September 1939 - June 1940
Tomahawk I/II Combat Log - European Theatre, 1941-42
Fortress MK.I Combat Log - Bomber Command High Altitude Bombing Operations, July-September 1941
F-84 Thunderjet - Republic Thunder
XF-92 - Convairs Arrow

www.ingramcontent.com/pod-product-compliance
Lightning Source LLC
Chambersburg PA
CBHW041702160426
43191CB00003B/53